Valerie Elaine Pettis

Mark Gett Leider

Sea House Press LLC
P.O. Box 633
Clinton, CT 06413

smeagulltheseagull.com

ISBN 978-1-7321929-0-4

Unabridged edition 2018

2 4 6 8 10 9 7 5 3 1

Book and cover design: Valerie Elaine Pettis
pettisdesign.com

Color scans: Profiles, profilesstudio.com

Drawings were created in pastel on colored paper.
Typeset in Glypha and Syntax

Printed in South Korea by Pacom Korea, Inc.

Sea House Press

For wild animals, wild places

and children everywhere.

Smeagull the Seagull

A TRUE STORY

By Mark Seth Lender   Illustrated by Valerie Elaine Pettis

There's a house near a seawall
Facing the shore,
And that house has a porch
With a sliding glass door.

And the people who live there, Valerie and me,

Stand by that door

And look toward the sea,

Because Smeagull the Seagull
Knows that we know,

He comes in the rain,

He comes in the snow,

He comes in the summer,

I'm telling the truth,

He comes when icicles
Hang from the roof!

He comes in the spring,

He comes in the fall,

He comes when it's cloudy

And there's no sun at all.

Yes, every day
At quarter past four,
Smeagull the Seagull
Knocks on the door!

He knocks when he's hungry,
He's hard to ignore,
It's Smeagull the Seagull
Asking for more!

Again in the morning at ten past six,

Smeagull comes knocking,

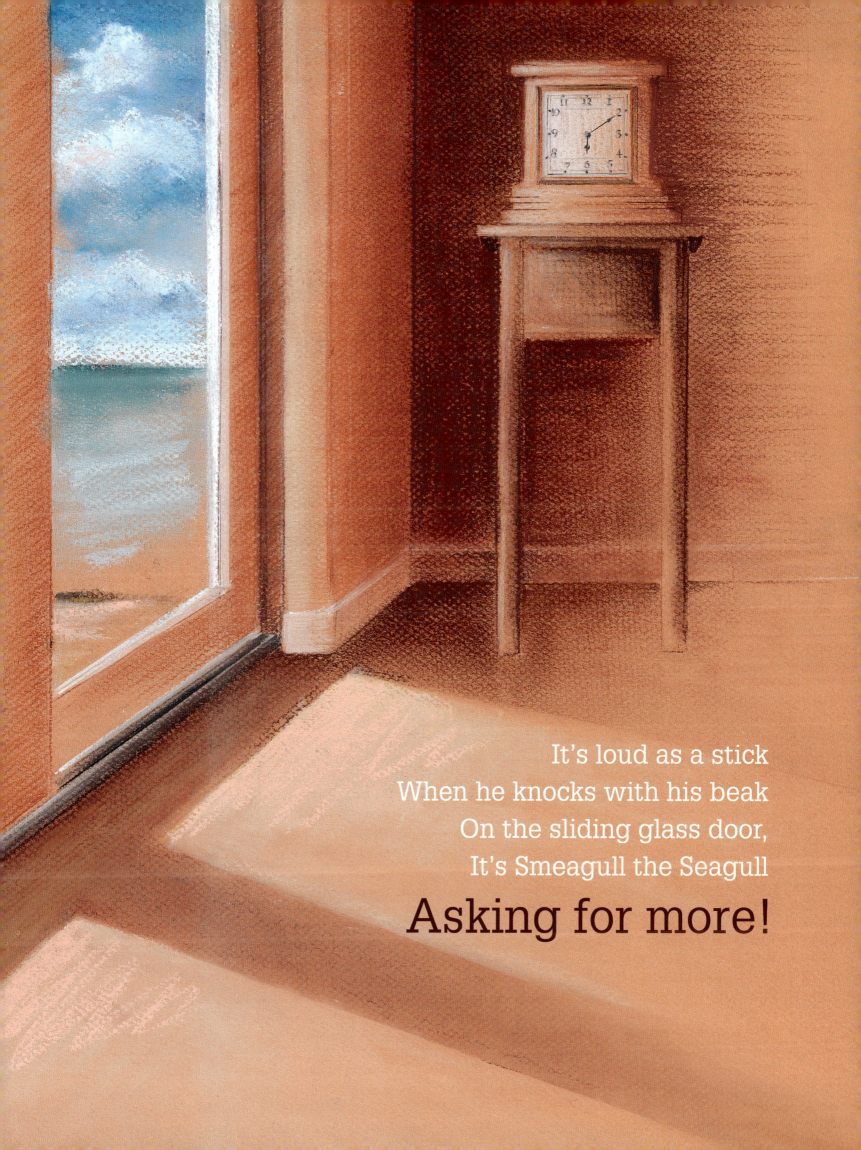

It's loud as a stick
When he knocks with his beak
On the sliding glass door,
It's Smeagull the Seagull
Asking for more!

Wherever you live, Seagull is heard,
It's spoken by Smeagull and millions of birds!

I can say, "I'm tired,
And I'm going to bed."

I can say, "I'm hungry,
And I want to be fed."

I can say, "I'm Angry,
Angry and Mad!"

I can say, "Please?"

I can say, "I'm so sad..."

Some people think they're
Smarter than birds,
But can they speak Seagull?

Not one single word.

I was talking and talking, I was all out of breath,
So I started knocking. Knocking works best.
My people know when I knock on the door,

It's Smeagull the Seagull
And I'm here for more!

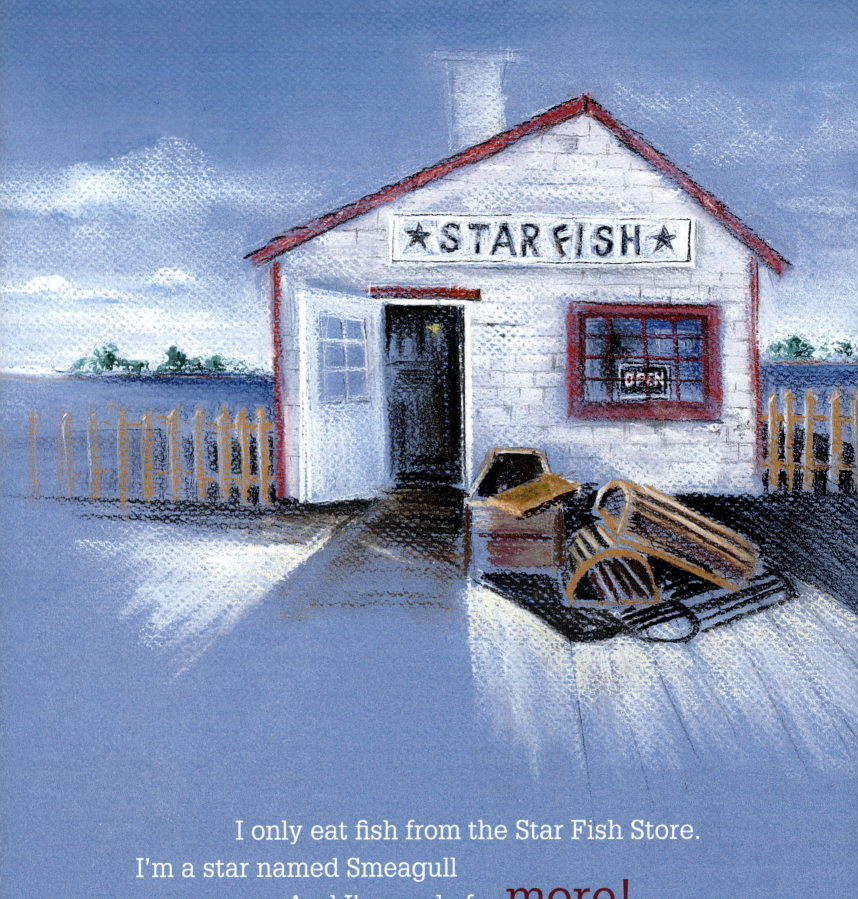

I only eat fish from the Star Fish Store.
I'm a star named Smeagull
          And I'm ready for more!

Smeagull the Seagull
    Walks down the beach,
He lands on the seawall,
    He flies out of reach.

All of the children all over town
Say, "There goes Smeagull!

Smeagull's around!"

All that walking and flying keeps Smeagull fit,

But it does make him hungry, and he eats quite a bit.

Shopping List

Sardines
Smelts
Oysters
Mussels
Mackerel
(local only!)

Treats:
Fried Clams

SMEAGULL

So we bought a new freezer
With a really big shelf,
Full of fish for Smeagull,
It's all for himself!
It stands in the kitchen
From ceiling to floor,
We thought we'd be ready
When Smeagull said,

"More!"

Then Valerie cried, "Where's Smeagull's fish?
The shelf is empty!
There's no food in his dish!
Star Fish will be closing in a minute or two."

I said, "Start the pickup!"
Down the driveway we flew.

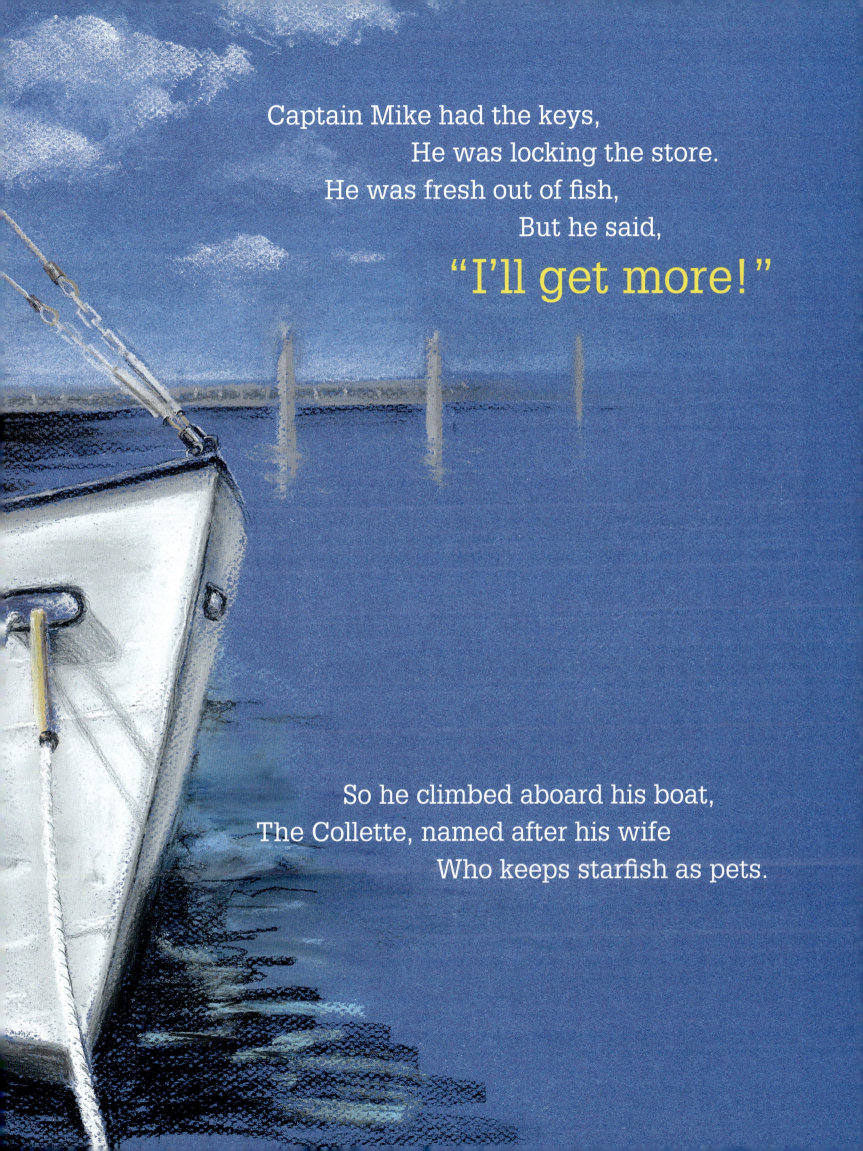

Captain Mike had the keys,
He was locking the store.
He was fresh out of fish,
But he said,
"I'll get more!"

So he climbed aboard his boat,
The Collette, named after his wife
Who keeps starfish as pets.

"Don't worry," he said, "we're not finished yet,
I'll head out to sea, and see what I get."
The engine roared, he was soon out of sight,
"If we have to," we called,

"We'll wait here all night!"

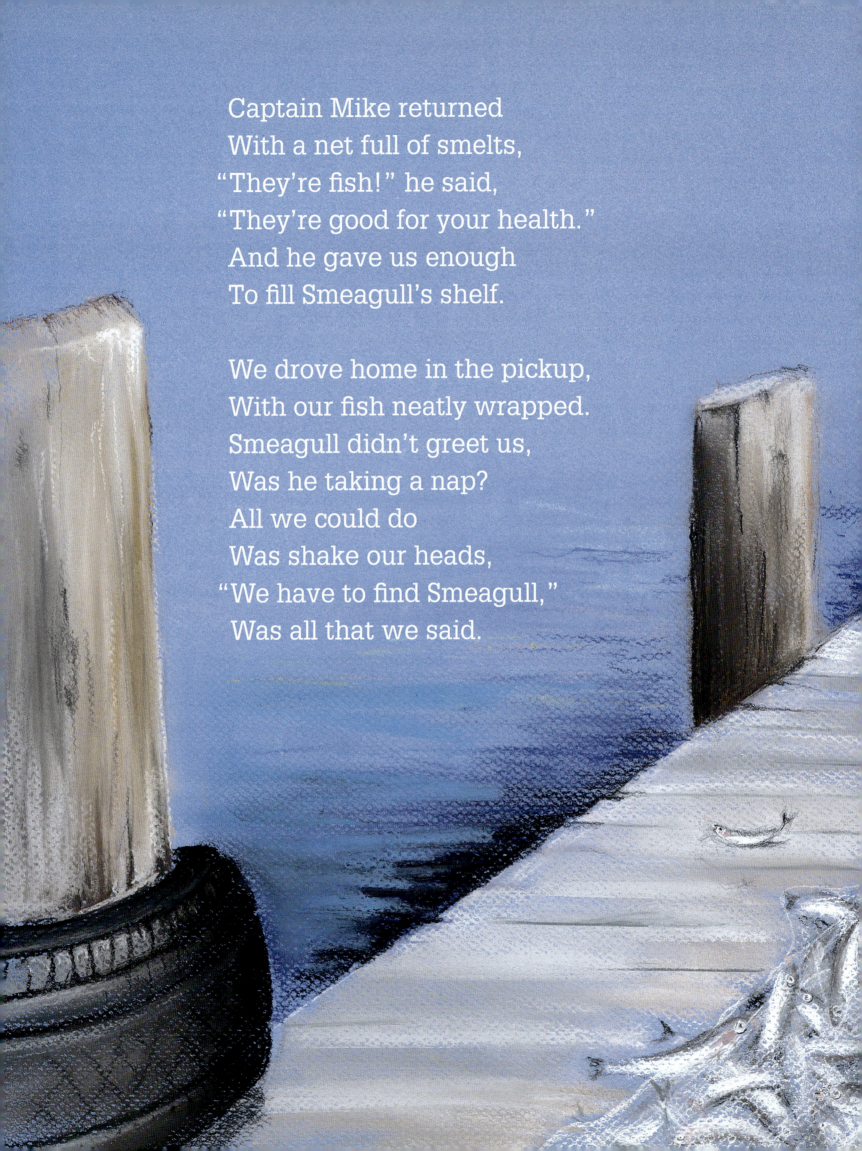

Captain Mike returned
With a net full of smelts,
"They're fish!" he said,
"They're good for your health."
And he gave us enough
To fill Smeagull's shelf.

We drove home in the pickup,
With our fish neatly wrapped.
Smeagull didn't greet us,
Was he taking a nap?
All we could do
Was shake our heads,
"We have to find Smeagull,"
Was all that we said.

All of the children all over the town,
Helped look for Smeagull.
They looked up. They looked down.
They looked in the trees.
They looked on the ground...

But Smeagull the Seagull

Was not to be found.

We were tired and hungry, but we couldn't eat.
        We turned off the lights, but we couldn't sleep.
It was cold and windy, and day after day,
        We waited for Smeagull, but he'd gone away.

        The sea cannot hear you. The sky cannot speak.

Life without Smeagull
Is lonely and bleak.

But what is that sound I hear at the door?
That knock, it's familiar. We ran 'cross the floor!

I'm Smeagull the Seagull. I'm back with my seagull.
Her name is She-gull, she's a seagull, like me.
There's an egg in our nest, and we'll soon be

A Family of Three!

There used to be one gull,
And now there are three gulls!
Smeagull, She-gull and baby gull, Me-gull!

Breakfast is served!

Flight practice 2.0

Smeagull teaching Me-gull to speak Seagull

I am born!

They're our Family Birds,

Me-gull's first step

And we love them

Too much for words.

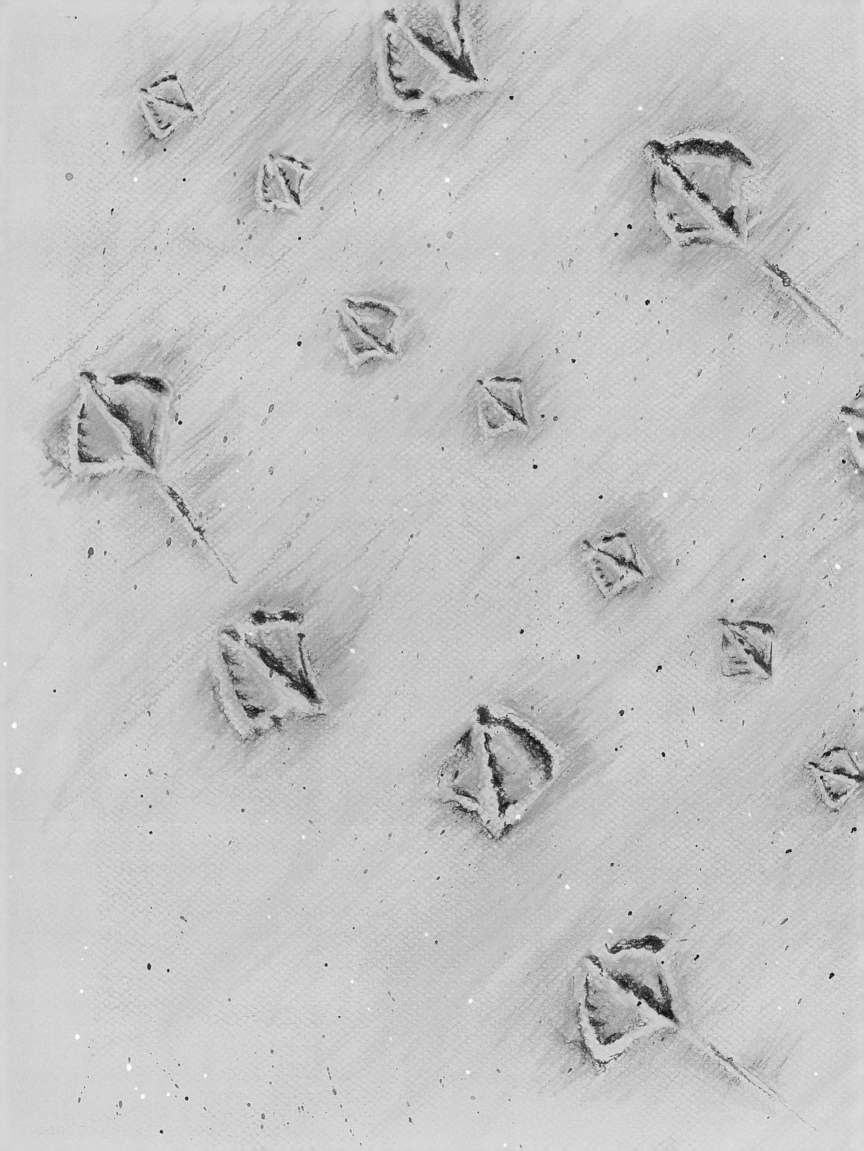